IVAN THE TERRIBLE

A Ruthless Leader

THE HISTORY HOUR

HISTORY

CONTENTS

❧ I ❧

INTRODUCTION

✦

There have been some wicked, ruthless leaders over time. Their nations have suffered as they pursued their own corrupted agendas. Surely, though, none comes close to the violent, lascivious, vengeful reign of **Ivan Chetvyorty Vasilyevich**, born to the **Rurik Dynasty** in the Grand Duchy of Muscovy. Indeed, this man's period in power was one of the longest in Russian history, lasting more than half a century. If the early years of his rule saw him as just a child, powerless to stop the corruption of his supposed mentors, he more than made up for it when coming of age. And Russia suffered as a result.

✦

He was also the first Tsar of this great country. A title he endowed upon himself which, as we shall later see, carried much greater significance to the Russian people than those four small letters might suggest.

This is a man whose reign went unrecorded - the fear of putting in writing anything he said or did is far too great to entertain. Thus, his history is told through stories passed down through generations, legends which have entered into folklore. If his history is therefore subject to the variations wrought by time, and the passions and fear he generated, one fact does stand tall and true. That is that we know this tyrant by a more memorable name.

Ivan the Terrible. Perhaps the most understated title in the history of mankind.

Even there, we see the duplicity which surrounds this leader. Undoubtedly he was savage, merciless and for much of his life completely tyrannical, but '***Terrible***' is unlikely to have been a moniker he would tolerate. At least, as we understand the word in the west. The term '***Terrible***' is a loose translation of the Russian word Grozny (in Russian, he is known as Ivan Grozny) – a term whose English counterpart is closer to the word '***formidable***' than '***terrible***.' Or perhaps even a third translation is one he would choose to apply: Like his forebear, Ivan the Great is a title that would appeal to his vanity.

It is certainly true that Ivan, official title **Ivan IV**, was Great in the range of his evil deeds, and Formidable in disposing of any who stood in his way. Or, unfortunately for his victims, he feared might one day stand in his way. Or even just vaguely suspected might not be one hundred percent behind him. Simply being in the wrong place at the wrong time was frequently enough to earn his ire. Indeed, our story will show that while the common translation applied to his sobriquet is far from perfect, it is the most appropriate we have.

Ivan the Terrible conducted a forty-year war against a hated foe. That war was not against some invading army, some political system with which he was opposed or even the extreme reaction to some long-lived family feud.

Ivan's war was against Russia itself, the country of which he was a leader. The tens, or maybe hundreds, of thousands who died at his hands, often as a direct result of his actions, were frequently his people. If the most hated, feared and psychotic leaders of history should be called tyrants, he took tyranny to new, unbelievable levels. He developed his own, personalized torture chamber. Prisoners were flayed, slashed and even more bizarrely boiled until their flesh dropped off – he also fried a foe or two on occasions. The agony he placed upon those who angered him – and frequently not even that – would, if their story appeared in some horror novel, be dismissed as being too far fetched to hold any link to reality.

Certainly, the sixteenth century was a time when vicious punishments were commonplace and torture an almost everyday occurrence, but Ivan went much further than that. His merciless deeds exceeded the extremes of any other despot throughout known history.

And that is strange because Ivan the Terrible was a committed Christian, whose own interpretation of the teachings of God justified, in his mind, the most callous and cruel of his actions. If Christianity is about love and forgiveness, these were elements of the religion which carried no weight in the eyes of the ruler of, in its time, the biggest country in the world.

BIRTH OF A TYRANT

«It's gettin'
    It's gettin'
    It's gettin' kinda heavy.
    I've got the power!»

Ivan the Terrible

Ivan was born in 1530. His father was Vasily III, a man not remiss himself when it came to carrying out what he needed to do to deliver the power he wanted. After his father, Ivan III's, death power went to another son, the originally named Ivan the Younger. But following this man's rapid demise Vasily seized the throne, becoming Grand Duke of Moscow in 1505.

If our personalities are rooted in the genes we inherit, then there may be some excuse for the man Ivan the Terrible became. Because his father too was possessed of vile moods and a vicious temper. This was not an unusual trait among past Russian Grand Dukes. Perhaps a life of absolute power, where the slightest whim is met with unquestioning acquiescence, contributed to this. But if Russian Princes led by fear many are recorded as possessing other, more positive, traits. Russia is a vast nation; physically and climatically it is as diverse as can be imagined. By the beginning of the 16th century, it was one of the strongest nations in the world. That does not happen by accident. It comes about through good, firm but forward-thinking leadership. Sadly, this was something Vasily did not possess in abundance. He was simply a bully.

❧❦❧

And a childless one throughout most of his life. He married Solominiya Saburova, but the two were unable to conceive. With no heir on the horizon, and the prospect of the centuries-old dynasty of which he was the latest, and possibly final, incarnation dying with him, he divorced the unfortunate Solominiya and married Elena (sometimes written Yelena), the daughter of a fellow prince. They had two children. Neither are served well by history. The younger, Yury, was born deaf. It will not surprise many that any kind of physical or mental defect was seen as unbecoming in a member of the aristocracy back in that day. However, Yury enjoyed the patronage of his only brother – a rare thing indeed, since that brother was none other than Ivan the Terrible. Indeed, while some interpretations of his life suggest that Yury was '*feeble-minded*,' it seems unlikely that this was the case. For a short time, while his brother was away fighting with the army, he took full control of state affairs. He also married and was a father to a son, albeit one who died in infancy.

❧

Ivan was just three years old when his father died. Vasily developed a sore on his leg which in turn became an abscess. The infection spread and painful death was endured. That death threw Russia into turmoil. With the heir still a baby, others – the Boyar – fought for supremacy. Elena herself battled to be accepted as regent, but when Ivan was still but a small boy, just eight years old, she too died. Elena was poisoned. It was a means of death that would come back to haunt Ivan much later in his life.

THE BOYARS – RUSSIA'S CORRUPT ELITE

A brief diversion to visit the Boyars is now due. This is the term given to the numerous families of Russian nobility. They were an unimpressive lot. Like hyenas around the bountiful gift that was Russia, they fought and schemed to grab the largest share and sit closest to the head. When that bountiful beast, in the form of Vasily, died, they flew into a frenzy of feeding, fighting tooth and nail to become, so to speak, top hyena.

Not all the Boyars were so inclined; self-interest did not occupy the waking thoughts of every member of this long-established aristocracy but loyal, well-meaning nobles were few and far between.

Ivan might be Grand Prince, but his childhood was wrought by terror. Both he and his brother were severely mistreated by the Boyars. And while the home was a Kremlin palace, the term *'prison'* might describe the conditions in which they existed more aptly. Armed men bestrode the corridors. As rival factions battled for supremacy, the boy never became more than a tool to deliver power to some ambitious Boyar or other, and often an obstacle that stood in the way of them.

❦

Fundamentally, the battle for power came down to an increasingly bloody conflict between two great families of Russian nobility - the Shuisky and the Belsky clans. Ivan and his younger brother became pawns in this feud, alternately courted for their support, then beaten, robbed and abuse, but never killed. It is hard to determine why.

❦

But if the boys survived, their closest confidents did not. The more ruthless of the two sides, the Shuiskys, began to gain the upper hand. Then, in 1539, they launched a raid on the palace and rounded up the majority of Ivan's remaining loyal servants. The most trusted of these, Fyodor Mishurin, was skinned alive and left in a square in Moscow to serve as both a warning and a target for abuse by the city's population.

❦

If childhood determines the man, then Ivan the Terrible's dreadful exploits as an impregnable ruler can be traced back to these early years. Parentless, unloved, with just a deaf younger brother as both friend and companion, Ivan threw himself into one field he found safe – the scriptures.

The conditions in which Ivan lived bordered on the inhuman. He was rarely given food; he was neglected. Sometimes he was abused. Physically, certainly. Maybe worse. Remember, his father had not been a well-liked leader so alongside the Boyar's battle for control of the country the emotion of revenge bubbled threateningly never far from the surface.

Indeed, given all of that, it is astonishing that young Ivan was not, as was the case with his mother, eliminated from the picture. But even though it never came to pass, that fate was one that was always just a sword length away. Physically neglected, emotionally humiliated, personally insecure, from the age of eight Ivan's childhood was a hellish as any could be imagined.

A CHILD OF GOD

৩৯৩

I f the adult Ivan was a man ridden with paranoia, it is not hard to see from where that condition originated. But despite it all, Ivan lived on. With no parents to protect him, he had to identify his protection as coming from somewhere. The answer slowly emerged to the boy. He was being protected by God. The greatest protection that could ever be offered. The seeds of megalomania were planted, and they would be watered by his continued mistreatment at the hands of the ambitious Boyars.

৩৯৩

The God of Ivan's experience was the ferocious one of the Old Testament; one who gained respect through fear, who ruled through retribution. The Old Testament is a bloody book; murders and massacres become everyday happenings. Vehemence and violence are the norms. And that bloody chaos looms God.

From this biblical source, the young Ivan learned many lessons. They were not ones we would wish upon a young, impressionable and scared child. Brutality and mercilessness, he came to believe, were the prerequisites of strength. If he was to survive, then he needed to be strong. There was just one person of any significance in his life – that was his younger, deaf, brother Yury. If he too was to survive the threats of the Boyars, then he would need an unflinching protector. Ivan determined to be that person.

A little historical perspective helps us to understand the power of young Ivan's faith. Today, the Russian Orthodox church still exists but is far from a mainstream source of spiritual guidance. But from the 15th Century, the opposite was the case. The Russian people saw their land as the center of Christianity. Their church was the true one, and therefore their leader was the voice of God on earth.

It is a powerful conceit and one which would appeal strongly to a neglected frightened young boy seeking a reason for his life. Was God testing him? Was he destined to be God's son on earth? It is easy to see how, locked away in his cold, harsh palace, such feelings could emerge, then multiply.

Once more, we can trace the man he became back to the boy that he was.

Ivan's devotion was obsessive. He would bang his head repeatedly on the stone floor before religious icons. So much so that he developed a callous on his forehead. This extreme belief celebrated through masochistic devotion would stay with him throughout his life.

Clearly, even as a child, Ivan was unstable. He would commit acts of sadistic cruelty on animals. Perhaps this obsession developed from the joy he gained from the self-inflicted suffering he endured through his extreme devotion to God. Or perhaps he murdered animals just because he enjoyed doing it.

Nevertheless, Ivan would take small animals – dogs, cats, young bears – to the top of the tower of his palace and throw them through the open window spaces to smash on the ramparts below.

We know from studies of sociopaths and psychotics today that their adult violence often grew from mistreatment of animals when they were a child. Ivan the Terrible would seem, on the face of it, a classic case which illustrates this behavior pattern. The vicious, sadistic killer of men he would become had its seeds in the violence he enjoyed committing on animals during his childhood.

❦

His torture of wildlife grew stronger. He would pluck the feathers from birds, then slash their stomachs open. It was as though every frustration in his small body was exorcized through his treatment of helpless creatures. It seemed as though holding their defenseless forms in his hands thrilled him in a way nothing else could.

❦

Over these small creatures, he was God. He decided whether they lived or died. And, he chose the means of their demise.

A CHILD'S BID FOR POWER

❧❧❧

But then, in 1539, the thirteen-year-old Ivan made his move. For all his savagery, he was a studious, well-read boy and enough was enough. It was time to act against the Boyars. On December 29th he invited the Shuiskys to dinner and there launched a sudden and savage verbal attack against their leader, Prince Andrew Shuisky. Another corrupted and cruel Prince of Russia was about to meet his end.

❧❧❧

Ivan had him arrested and summarily thrown to a pack of hunting dogs. These had been starved in preparation for this event and trapped in a secure enclosure. They quickly found their prey. Ivan, the cruel but neglected boy, turned overnight into a leader in his own right. And now that cruelty which was a defining part of his personality could flourish unchecked.

Many of the horrors Ivan would go on to inflict can be traced back to this time. Now it was humans he targeted, not animals. Even if helplessness remained a characteristic of his victims. But despite the power the thirteen-year-old now enjoyed, effectively unchallenged, he was still a child and a very disturbed one at that.

Alcohol became his drug of choice – perhaps it dampened down the terrors of his younger days. He gained a gang of similarly aged followers who began to terrorize the streets of Moscow. Soon, vandalism turned to assault. It was not long before that crime escalated to rape. In foresight of the reign of terror to come, there was no mercy shown to the victims he and his cohorts attacked.

Women and girls were hung, thrown to bears and sometimes buried alive.

Soon Ivan discovered a new past time. He gained a love of hunting. It legitimized his continued pleasure of inflicting pain and suffering on animals. But soon the Grand Prince was satiated with the joys of hunting boar and bears. He turned his attention to a more intelligent branch of the animal world, and farmers became his next prey. He would rob them and inflict upon them savage beatings. No doubt, many died at his hands. Indeed, on one occasion, he set his hounds on one of his servants, a member of his household who was still just a boy.

⚜

The Russian people were powerless to stop him. But through all this violence and cruelty, the young Ivan continued in his devotions to God. They remained as extreme as those prayers he performed as a young child. If anything, his practice was more obsessional. He would still throw himself before icons and beat his head against stone walls, wooden pillars, and floors. On one occasion, he even carried out a public confession in Moscow. That must have made an interesting, if somewhat debased, watch.

⚜

By his mid-teens, Ivan was a complex mixture of extremes. Paranoid and savage embittered and vengeful, brutal but brutalized. If ever there was a perfect example of a young psychopath, then the most powerful man in the then biggest nation in the world fitted that unwanted bill. And like the most disturbed members of any society, he was exhilarated by the power he wielded, but also too quickly satisfied by it. Wider and wider sensory stimulation was required to meet his needs. This is not unusual in psychopaths – it is just that mostly these people are not born into positions of supreme power.

RUSSIA'S DREAM – AT LAST,
A TSAR

But for all his madness – it is not possible to draw any other conclusion about this tyrant's mental state – Ivan was an intelligent young man, well read and learned. As he approached his seventeenth birthday, he realized that he needed to cement his position at the top of the Russian pyramid of power. In January of 1547, Ivan announced his forthcoming coronation. Not, it should be noted, was the coronation announced by some third party – it was an action he decided upon himself. His father had been known as Grand Prince, a title he too had taken.

But that was not enough for a megalomaniacal psychopath. His God complex came to the fore, and he announced he would become the Tsar of Russia.

This term comes from the Roman, appropriately enough in Ivan's case, for Caesar. The boy claimed direct descendancy from Rome, and as such he would rule supreme over all houses of nobility. The position had not previously existed, and it is highly unlikely that he was in any way descended from Roman aristocracy. But a requirement for truth was not something held in particularly high esteem by Ivan. Frankly, since there was nobody prepared to challenge the child's power, he was able to think what he wished and act on his every whim.

For the Boyars, Ivan's idea was bad news indeed (which may, in part, have been why he decided upon it). The title Tsar gave the holder sacred power over them – their influence would be instantly diminished. But as we have seen, Ivan was a clever, if wicked, leader. He understood that the Russian people were sick themselves of the corruption, the warring, the exploitation of the Boyars. They longed for a man they could call King. In Ivan, for all his manifold faults, they had found one.

❧ III ☙

A MENAGERIE OF MARRIAGES

«Sometimes I'm not sure what I hate more...everyone or everything...»

Ivan the Terrible

At this point, the young man's story enters a realm which is a mixture between fairy tale and gutter TV. He announced that he would take a Russian bride – something further guaranteed to please his people – and would hold a national virgin competition to find the woman he would marry. It was 1542 and Russia was entering a period of rapid change.

AN INFLUENCE FOR GOOD

Girls aged twelve and above were paraded in front of him; some estimates put the figure at 1500. He made his choice – Anastasia Romanovna – no doubt after long and careful consideration. Despite the somewhat populist nature of the selection process to find his bride, it was hardly a meritocratic process. Anastasia was herself the child of wealthy boyars, although distinctly second-tier members of the aristocratic Houses of Russia.

It may even be the case that the two had already met. Anastasia's uncle was one of the guardians who had guided Ivan between the death of his parents.

However, for whatever reason, Anastasia was his chosen bride and astonishingly, given the dubious nature of its origins, and the even more dubious nature of the husband in the partnership, it was a marriage that flourished, marking the sanest and most controlled period of Ivan's life since the death of his mother.

❦

Indeed, the boy turned into a calmer, more tolerant (relatively speaking) man once his life was filled with proper love once more. This gives some support to the argument that his anger and volatility was learned through his appalling childhood experiences, rather than inherited through some dubious family gene.

❦

Learned behavior can be controlled, inherited conditions less so. Anastasia and Ivan enjoyed thirteen years of marriage. Despite its uncertain origins, it does appear as though there was genuine love between the two. Together, they had six children although all but two died in infancy.

❦

But it was Anastasia's character which seemed to pass a benign effect on her volatile husband. She was able to laugh, and put matters into context, and this approach rubbed off on Ivan. The devout man who spent much of his childhood and early adulthood bouncing between personal flagellation for his sins and handing out torture and death to his citizens was calmed.

Even if Russia continued to fight on many fronts for a short period internal tensions were eased.

A COUNTRY UNIFIED...AND
DIVIDED

I f matters were better, they remained far from perfect. In the year following Ivan's coronation, Moscow fell victim to an inordinately high number of fires. Many were killed in the destruction, while even more were made homeless.

With no obvious target to blame, Ivan took the responsibility for the fires onto himself. They were, he decided, a punishment from God for his neglect of his kingdom. Ivan prostrated himself in a Moscow square, swearing to protect his people. It is a part of the complexity of the man that, despite the unbelievable horrors that he enacted on a subdued people, he took spiritual responsibility for any failure – perceived or otherwise – that came his way.

He could be in no way blamed for the fires that hit the city, but still, he took it upon himself to carry the burden for the destruction they caused – spiritually, if not physically.

Nevertheless, the fires led to reform. Ivan's way of addressing the message God had sent to him was to change the order of society. He reformed the church and the army. He withdrew power from the Boyars – a nobility already partially castrated under his rule. In enacting these changes, he modernized Russian society. It became unified under him. Something that would have been to Russia's long-term advantage had Ivan been a more stable and empathetic man.

He was a man of God, one closer to God than any other. Therefore, since God was good, so must he be. And that goodness needed to be enjoyed by others. Forcibly if necessary.

THE TAKING OF KAZAN

❧❧❧

He invaded and conquered the Muslim enclave of
Kazan, which lay to the East of Moscow, declaring
the success a religious victory. This was an important triumph, both for his popularity and strategic advantage.

❧❧❧

Throughout recent history, constant invasions by the Tartars
had occurred. These incursions were damaging to moral as
well as to the lives and wealth of the Russians they
encountered.

❧❧❧

Tartar control of Kazan, a town on the Volga, had prohibited
use of that mighty river as a route to the Caspian Sea, from
which access (and therefore trade) could be found to other
nations. In 1552, following careful preparations, the Russian

army attacked the town and seized it. When, four years later, the final Tartar stronghold on the Volga, Astrakhan, fell without a fight, the Volga became a Russian river, and the route to the Caspian Sea was secured.

He also understood that if Russia was to be the dominant world force that God had decided it should be, then it needed to communicate beyond its borders.

Opening the route to the Caspian Sea had been an important step on this path. Now Ivan opened trading links with the West, Britain. His marriage to Anastasia was delivering a golden age for the country.

But golden ages have a habit of ending suddenly, with all the glory and joy of their times disappearing in a flash. Such an occurrence happened in 1560 when Ivan was thirty years old. One, deeply significant, event changed the country. Because it changed Ivan. For the worse.

He beloved, dear and calming Anastasia died. And Ivan feared that her death was the result of the foulest of play.

DEATH OF A PRINCESS; MURDER
OF A NATION

There was no obvious explanation for Anastasia's death. Although she was just twenty-six years of age, and in the prime of her life, she fell victim to a long illness and one from which she would never recover.

But people do fall prey to disease. Often ones unexplained by the extremely limited knowledge of medicine man held in the 1500s. There were many possible causes that could have led to Anastasia's untimely demise. But to Ivan, there was no doubt about the cause of his beloved's death. She had been poisoned. And equally, he had no qualms in deciding on the perpetrators of his wife's murder. It was the Boyars, finally taking the cruelest form of revenge for his curtailment of their powers.

Despite his conclusions, he had no evidence to back them up. Still, evidence was an optional luxury when it came to dispensing justice under the Tsar's rule.

But before we see how Anastasia's death did lead to the rightful addition of '**_The Terrible_**' to her husband's name, we shift forward in time for nearly five hundred years.

It has been passed in the legend that Anastasia was poisoned, but only because those were the words that Ivan ordered. However, researchers looking at life in the Kremlin's distant pass made a discovery which pointed without doubt to the fact that Ivan's deduction was correct. Most probably, that was due to paranoia infested chance rather than good detective work. Or perhaps somebody did confess to knowing the truth about Anastasia's demise. This person could well have been enduring the most agonizing of tortures at the time and was desperately welcoming the death which awaited next door. He would undoubtedly be encouraging it to enter the torture chamber and embrace him. But none of that means that his confession lacked truthfulness.

However, modern science has demonstrated that the Tsaritsa was indeed poisoned, and the drug of choice which brought about her death was that doyen of detective stories, mercury. When this metal is ingested, the kidneys battle hard to expel it, and the body excretes as much as the poison as it can through urine and sweat. However, its deadly effects still take hold, and death is a certainty while the poisoning continues. Some of the substance remains within the body and continues to do its damage. The outcome is rarely in question.

Scientists examined the body of Anastasia preserved in the Kremlin and made the discovery that her hair retained large amounts of mercury, most likely transmitted there through sweat. Certainly, sixteenth-century make-up tended to contain plenty of deadly metal and led to the untimely death of many women. However, insufficient quantities could be absorbed through the skin to produce the amount of the substance found in Anastasia's hair.

The same scientists made a further discovery. Elena, Ivan's mother, had also been poisoned with the same killer chemical. That mercury was used in the deaths, nearly a quarter of a century apart, of the two closest women Ivan ever knew or loved, is too much of a coincidence to ignore.

While it always seemed certain that the Boyars were behind the death of Elena, committed in pursuit of their ambitions, now it seems the strongest probability that they were also the killers of Anastasia.

Their motivations this time would have been two-fold. Firstly, for revenge against Ivan's past actions. Secondly, the death of his beloved wife would push the unstable Tsar back over the edge of sanity into the madness that lay so close to his surface. It was a risky strategy in the extreme, but one that Ivan correctly, we now know, detected.

The impact on Russia was catastrophic. Without Anastasia, there was not any kind of mediating influence on Ivan. He could conduct his policies as he wished, with no thought to the consequences they caused.

While there was undoubtedly resentment towards him from some of the Boyars, mostly the families of the nobility were loyal. They fought in his armies and supported his policies. That now counted for nothing. Thirty years of anger was bottled up inside of him, and suddenly the stopper was removed. With no calming wife, there was nobody able to staunch the flow of violence which poured forth.

The Boyars were the first victims. Children, women, servants, princes, noblemen – nobody was spared from the torture. Boys as young as twelve were subject to the same agonies that their fathers endured until they finally passed away from their pain and indignity. A storm of terror was unleashed, and nothing provided shelter from it.

A simple logic infiltrated Ivan's mind. God had allowed his Anastasia to be taken. That was the act of a cruel and unthinking soul. If God acted in this way, then the message he was sending to his apostle on earth was the same. Ivan too must rule cruelly, and irrationally.

SEEKING A NEW QUEEN – A
SUCCESSION OF MARRIAGES

Whether in any way it was a recognition that a wife brought a calming influence on him, Ivan attempted to replicate the relationship he had enjoyed. He married no less than seven times following Anastasia's death. Or maybe he married so often to satiate his lecherous sexual proclivity. Whichever is the more truthful alternative, that a high number of marriages gives evidence of the dissatisfaction these wives caused him. Or, perhaps, they tell us that nothing could live up to his Anastasia.

The first woman to attempt to fill the shoes of his deceased beloved was Maria Temryukovna. This relationship lasted a reasonable amount of time. Maria changed her name and converted to Christianity to meet the Tsar's wishes. She married him on 21st September 1561, just two months after her religious conversion.

❦

Their marriage lasted for eight years, but she died in 1569. Rather like his first wife, the rumors were that Maria was poisoned. But there the similarities between her and Anastasia stopped. Maria had been around just sixteen years of age (her date of birth is impossible to certify) when she married Ivan. Already, though, she was wild tempered and mean spirited. For Ivan, it had been her beauty that had been her attraction. Anastasia had warned him to beware of Pagans – it seemed good advice, since, despite her conversion to Christianity, Maria was hated by her subjects and, very quickly, by Ivan himself. He regarded her as too ungentrified to fit into Moscow life, and her illiteracy put further distance between the two. Indeed, some stories put forward the idea that it was Ivan himself who poisoned her. If it was, his torture of numerous suspects following her death would have proved to be an unnecessary cover for an act to which he would never have to answer.

❦

Together they bore a son, Vasyli, but he died as an infant. Probably, her main contribution to his life was that it was she, according to many sources, who encouraged Ivan to create his oprichniki, more about which we learn later.

❦

Next to come along was Marfa Sobakina...and she was soon to pass on. Ivan was still fond of choosing his wives X-Factor style, and selected Marfa from twelve '*finalists*.' Unfortunately, her mother persuaded her to drink a potion which would increase her fertility, but instead of helping her to conceive, it promptly poisoned her. Within a few days of her betrothal, she too was dead.

Perhaps her most significant impact on Ivan's life was to make him even more paranoid than usual. Convinced that she had been poisoned within the safe walls of his fortress, he set about torturing and executing many of his court, including his former brother in law, Mikhail Temrjuk. Mikhail had been a huge and positive influence on his life, one who had guided Ivan through many of the best reforms he made. His good advice lost as a result of Ivan's uncontrollable temper would be something the tsar would never replace.

Never one to take a hint of any kind, and certainly not that marriage might not be for him. Ivan sought wife number four. The next unfortunate to earn his hand was Anna Koltovskaya. This particular liaison nearly failed to materialize. That was thanks to the Russian Orthodox church, which decreed a fourth marriage to be an impiety.

With the skills of a seasoned politician, Ivan got around that particular hurdle by announcing that he had not consummated his third marriage. Presumably, he could just as easily use his self-professed position as God's agent on earth by simply marrying anyway. It is unlikely anybody would raise too many objections. At least, not if they valued their lives.

However, this time he acquiesced to the Church's demands. The prelates required that he spend time with penitents; whether or for how long he adhered to that requirement we do not know. The happy couple honeymooned in Novgorod, which only two years before he had ransacked. No doubt that made him a less than welcome guest.

The marriage was doomed to failure. Anna Koltovskaya did not conceive, and he committed her to a monastery. (A move he had enacted on wives of his son who failed to bear human fruit.)

The production line continued. Next came Anna Vasilchikova. Little is known about Anna. Ivan decided to forego the church side of the marriage altogether this time. The two were not married for long. Again, she did not immediately bear him a child, so she found herself rapidly dispatched to a monastery. Within a year, this latest of the Tsaritsas was dead.

Vasilisa Melentyeva was the penultimate wife Ivan the Terrible chose to take. Or maybe she was not. Some uncertainty surrounds Vasilisa. She may have been a widow when they married, or they may not have ever formalized their liaison. That's the problem when little written records remain of a tyrant's reign. There is a lot of sitting on the fence.

The story is that the Tsar found this wife to be kind and sweet tempered. Perhaps, in this, she was most like his beautiful Anastasia. However, he is also said to have discovered that she was having an affair with a Russian prince. He immediately executed the amorous royal, making Vasilisa watch her lover's slow and painful death. She was then cast into a palace cloister, where she remained until death.

But there are many inconsistencies surrounding Vasilisa. The lack of records regarding her marriage to Ivan puts, in some historian's eye, Vasilisa's entire being into doubt. On the other hand, if she did marry the Tsar, it was without the Church's blessing. Hence the lack of written proof of their liaison.

Lack of a marriage record does not seem conclusive evidence of her non-existence. After all, the church had also failed to bless his previous marriage, and number four had only been granted after a struggle.

Other historians conclude that Vasilisa was a concubine who passed briefly through the Tsar's life. She would not be the first or last if that is the case.

But the evidence supporting any marriage she had with the Tsar is also flimsy. There are only two mentions of her in

Russian history books. The first simply lists her in passing as a prostitute. The main record of her existence was written by Alexander Sulakadzev. Unfortunately, he is not a reliable source; his writings -made in the early 1800s - having been exposed as fraudulent.

❦

Whether she existed or not, there is neither reliable record of her time as Ivan's wife, nor is there a grave or memorial to her, at least not one that has yet been found and identified.

❦

Last and very possibly least of the Tsar's official betrothals was to Maria Nagaya. Once more, the Orthodox Church was excluded from the process, Ivan by now feeling he had a direct line to God. To be fair to poor Maria, while she was anything but one of Ivan's favorites, by the time they married in 1581 his health was fading, he was most probably suffering from rheumatoid arthritis and very likely a host of other conditions. To say he was rarely the most affable of people is an understatement of enormous proportions but by this point in his life, he was at his most ferociously volatile.

❦

That Maria remained his wife until his death is a testament to her staying powers...and the fact that she did bear him a son. To give an idea of the low regard in which she was held by the tsar, he contacted Queen Elizabeth in London, offering to abandon Maria to marry the Queen's cousin. The kind offer was rejected. By this point, Ivan the younger was dead, and Ivan IV had little faith in his younger son, Feodor. So, the arrival of Dmitry in 1582 was a welcome relief, and probably saved Maria the fate that had befallen some of her predecessors – being cast out to a monastery.

However, as a sign of the dismissive manner he held towards her, Ivan left nothing to Maria in his will, and she was forced to live off the income of her infant son. He had been granted Uglich, a border town on the River Volga. Sadly, young Dmitry died from a seizure when still a small boy.

HEIRS TO A CORRUPTED
THRONE

෯ඥ෯

There were two other significant people in Ivan's life. His sons, Ivan and Feodor. Ivan was the favorite. Like his father, he was well read and savage. He enjoyed nothing more than to watch the oprichniki at their work. Once, a prisoner by the name of Bykovski seized a sword and raised it to attack Ivan senior. His son stepped in and stabbed the would-be assassin. It is deeply ironic, therefore, that the younger Ivan would eventually die at his father's hands.

෯ඥ෯

Ivan was set for marriage at the age of twelve to the daughter of the King of Sweden, Virginia Eriksdotter. That came to nothing, but he did wed at the age of seventeen...to one of the women his father had rejected when choosing his wife following Anastasia's death. The idea was to provide an heir, but when that did not happen the poor woman, Eudoxia was banished to a convent. She was soon joined, for the same reason, by Ivan's second wife, Praskovia Solova. Only by the third attempt, to Yelena Sheremeteva, would an heir be conceived.

❀

If Ivan was the favorite who shared many of his father's characteristics, then his younger brother Feodor certainly did not. Weak-willed, possibly intellectually disabled he bore none of the ambition of his father and brother. History records him as kind and gentle. He did continue the Rurik dynasty, which had ruled for centuries, after his father's death and did become Russia's second tsar.

❀

But Ivan the Terrible's true dynasty was unique to him – only his eldest son could have carried that forward. Indeed, despite ruling in name, when Feodor finally ascended to the throne, in practice the country was led by his brother-in-law.

❀

Feodor died childless, and Russia – already crumbling – fell into total disarray.

❧ IV ❧

A TYRANT'S AGONY

"I will not see the destruction of the christian converts who are loyal to me, and to my last breath I will fight for the orthodox faith."

Ivan the Terrible

However, there is yet another factor which contributed in some ways to the floods of violence Ivan IV undammed upon his people. That factor was his deteriorating physical health. We can be as sure as history allows that Ivan the Terrible was mentally unhinged. Most probably, that was largely a result of losing his mother at an early age, of never knowing his father and, on top of it all, experiencing a childhood of terror and fear, abused and neglected in equal amounts.

Given his father's erratic behavior, and the reputation of many for the Grand Princes who predated him, it is a not unreasonably leap of faith to conclude that his instability might also have been genetic.

ILLNESS OF THE BODY

❧

But we saw that under the influence of his much loved first wife he could control the excesses of his behavior. During that time, he pulled Russia together. The force of his will overcame dissent and distrust. He could act for good.

❧

As he got older, another influence was playing a cruel part in his own story, and that of his nation. Two closely loosely connected influences which led to a third, ironic situation which without a doubt added to his psychosis.

❧

Ivan the Terrible suffered from rheumatoid arthritis. Examinations of his remains carried out in the 1960s provided undeniable evidence of this. Rheumatoid arthritis is a debilitating condition. Even with today's arsenal of medicines and pain killers, it remains an agonizing disease. Imagine the endless pain reverberating through his body. His suffering would be worsened by the cold conditions of the long Russian winters. Such a state could only grate away at a damaged mind. Nobody, it would seem to him, could show more devotion to his God. That same God continued to punish him. It was a conundrum to which he could not come to terms.

It seems highly likely that Ivan also suffered from syphilis. The disease was rampant in sixteenth-century Russia, as indeed it was throughout much of the world. Sexually transmitted, most promiscuous were the most vulnerable to its unwanted and painful tentacles. Few were more promiscuous than Ivan the Terrible.

We know from his days as a youth that Ivan was driven by sexual desires. Those yearnings returned and flourished in his post-Anastasia adulthood.

Affairs, casual sex, rape, enslavement. All were regular pages in his life's story. And Ivan was not overly particular with regards to who it was unwillingly forced into his bedchamber. Men, boys, girls, women...his tastes were eclectic in the extreme. In such circumstances, it is hard to see how his body could not be riddled with sexually transmitted infections.

Symptoms of syphilis include tiredness, headaches, flu-like pains and discomfort in the joints. The disease can remain latent in a person, reappearing at regular intervals.

So, we find our violent, heartless and cruel leader with moods worsened by a combination of constant pain and a sense that God will not forgive him for whatever sins the Great Being has decided he has committed. As we saw earlier, medicines of 1540 were basic and generally prone to cause more harm than good. With a painful irony, Ivan could not have known at the time, one of the most common forms of medicine was also one of the most dangerous. For joint illness, a usual treatment was to prescribe mercury. The very poison that almost certainly killed his wife and mother was one he took himself in a failed attempt to relieve the constant pain from which he suffered.

We know, from the studies of his remains, that his body contained considerable amounts of mercury. Of course, this could be evidence of an attempt to poison him in the same way his wife and mother were dispatched, although this is a less likely probability than an effort to relieve his symptoms.

ILLNESS OF THE MIND

❧

But mercury does more than just poison the body. It alters the mind. Its effect on the brain can be catastrophic. It leads to violent mood swings and outbursts of irrational, uncontrollable temper. Here is a paranoid psychotic bearing the added burden of a poisoned mind. Such a combination offers some insight into the reasons for the savagery of his reign of terror.

❧

As we try to analyze the causes for the state of his mind, we see how complex this was. His extreme violence towards animals as a child is a common forerunner to extreme violence in adulthood. The raping, torturing and murdering that followed after he seized control as a thirteen-year-old is further evidence of a deeply disturbed mind. And back then he could not call on the defense of being poisoned by mercury. The period of relative calm which rippled outwards during his marriage to Anastasia proved that he could, under certain conditions, moderate his behavior.

But as an older man, his extreme violence would be followed by bouts of severe depression as he saw the consequences of his uncontrollable temper. These are not the traits we want to see in a leader. Particularly not when that leader is blessed with absolute, unquestioned, power. That authority could be seen in physical form in the long, ornate and deadly staff he always carried. A deadly weapon topped with a golden point capable of wounding...or killing. The picture of this despot is complete. It is not a pleasant one.

THE GREATEST GAMBLE

❦

I n 1565 the Tsar made the strangest of decisions. He announced that he would abdicate, that the trouble and unrest in the country was not the result of his megalomaniac behavior, but the result of sedition by the evil Boyars who sought to blight him (and his people) at every turn.

❦

The announcement was almost certainly made for political gain. Although it was a spur of the moment decision made in anger cannot be dismissed. Most modern historians believe that his announcement was to gain leverage with his people. He gambled on the belief that the townsfolk, the peasants and even the Boyar themselves could not contemplate a country without the figurehead of a tsar, as frightening as having one might be. As much as all feared him, so he was seen as indispensable by his people. Society is a strange beast.

As the population saw it, the choice facing them lay between tyranny and utter chaos.

That former alternative was, by most, seen as the marginally better choice of two terrible options.

Many could remember the corruption and catastrophes of the leaderless times when Ivan was still a child. As bad as the alternative was proving to be, a return to that chaos would undoubtedly be worse. So, the people chose to gather behind the tsar. His ploy had paid off. Senior members of the nobility, along with leading members of the clergy held a secret meeting, and from that elected to beg the tsar to continue as their leader.

Ivan agreed, but he had a price. The cost of his continued leadership was high. He wanted the right to a free hand to purge his country of anything he saw fit and to do so without fear of opposition or criticism. There are plenty who would argue that this was, in any case, what he was doing. But now he could carry out his purges officially, with a license to do so signed by more than just himself.

And that meant, to his twisted mind, that he was now the sole interpreter of the will of God. Effectively, he was God among his people.

But even a God needs someone to carry out his dirty work. Ivan's first step was to create his secret police, a personal bodyguard to undertake his every wish. He effectively cut the country into two. Russia is a vast mass of varied land. From ice covered wilderness, through to rich and fertile plains; from regions with unbearable variations in weather to others whose climate is the equal of any in the world. It is no surprise that these more temperate regions held the wealth of the country, while the other, bleaker outposts were populated by peasants.

Ivan had little interest in those poorer parts. To control them directly would place an enormous burden on his resources. So, as a convenient sop to the Boyars, he left them to run the most barren, most impoverished parts of the great country. Even then, those who survived paid a further price.

A recent archaeological discovery shed light onto one of the duties of the Boyars who were permitted to remain as a part of the Russian nobility. The find was a huge arsenal. The weapons contained within included bows, sabers and spears. Articles of uniform also survived, including the leather belts worn by the tsar's secret army and the pointed hats that adorned their heads.

The find was in an old wooden cellar, the house above it

having burned down centuries before. The weapons were perfectly preserved and unused. The implication was that the Boyars would be required to host squadrons of Ivan's version of the Gestapo, feeding and sheltering them as a standing unit who could head to war if called upon. Ivan the Terrible's military machine truly was complex and powerful.

THE OPRICHNIKI – THE TSAR'S SECRET POLICE

Meanwhile he, through this secret army called the oprichniki, directly ruled the richest regions. It was a rule marked by ruthless cruelty.

In many ways, Ivan the Terrible's regime echoed Russia of the Soviet Union some four hundred years later. The secret police of the communist regime of Stalin – the KGB – can be represented by his army of oprichniki.

This police were fearsome. Dressed all in black, they rode black horses which were decked out in the severed heads of dogs.

With a touch that would be humorous had these men not been so savage they carried brooms as symbols of their intent to sweep away any wrongs. Faults which, of course, were perceived as such by their leader. This frightening collection of men consisted of the most terrifying in Russia. Many were criminals of the most ruthless, heartless variety. Most were hand-picked by Ivan, who sought out the cruelest men he could find.

※

We used the term '*police*' earlier, but in reality, this was a misnomer. These were not up keepers of law and order. Not even laws generating from a government which used fear as its agent of control. They were legitimized criminals. Simply, they swept through the Russian countryside and towns, raping, stealing, killing. They took whatever they wanted. And did so with the authority of Ivan behind them.

※

But even in an organization as corrupted as the oprichniki a hierarchy exists. Ivan took the three hundred members of his secret police who he identified as the most vicious, most cut-throat and installed them as his guard in his palace. A palace which, with unknowing irony, he referred to as his '*monastery*.'

※

It was an astonishing place. In some ways, its practices did reflect those of a high church monastery. Ivan was still besotted by his devotion to God. It was just that his was a God that none would recognize; a threatening, evil creature who cast out plague and suffering on His people. And if it was good enough for God...then that was good enough for Ivan.

❦

Like some ultra-devout monastic residence, life at the palace ran to a tight schedule – one that was immeasurably harsh. Ivan himself would start the day at 3.00 am, ringing bells to summon his guard to the church for prayers. And each of those guards had better be ready to rise in the icy dark. Failure to attend prayers resulted in prison – not a place in which any would wish to spend time.

❦

The service that followed was little more than a performance to a captive audience. Ivan would sing, chant, beat himself and prostrate himself before his altar. This would continue for four hours. Sleep would follow, along with a short meal. Then, when the morning moved to the afternoon, the fun would begin.

❦

Ivan used this part of the day to visit his dungeons. Most frightening of all among these was Ivan's torture chamber. Within its walls he created hell. Punishment there was of biblical proportions. Those unfortunate enough to have encountered his wrath sufficiently to find themselves in this room could look forward to nothing but unimaginable suffering.

❦

Sometimes Ivan would be a thrilled observer to the torture that took place each afternoon; an excited member of the audience to the performance provided to entertain him. A show, of course, whose leading man (or woman, or child) would rather be anywhere else. At other times, Ivan took an active role in proceedings, casting himself as a torturer in chief. A witness from the time described how Ivan would leave the torture chamber smiling in contentment.

Perhaps, given an exceptionally tolerant viewpoint, the excessive religious observance of the mornings might be excused as an overzealous devotion to God. Even the afternoon's torture sessions could be viewed as a misplaced attempt to cleanse the world of evil. But the final part of a typical day at Ivan's palace was completely impossible to justify in even the broadest, most tolerant view of what constituted accepted the religious practice because the final excess of the day was a sexual one. An orgy, featuring unwilling peasants, girls, boys, women, forced to engage in the most bizarre of practices with Ivan and selected members of his secret police. Raped, whipped, sodomized – even used as live target practice these young unfortunates were pushed into hell. Often, they would never leave. At least, not whilst still alive.

Death was also an unwanted outcome facing landowners and Boyars who fell victim to the rampaging oprichniki. Conservative estimates put the number of victims killed by these warriors as 10000 – many more were forcibly evicted from their land and homes, which were, in turn, taken over by Ivan's marauding forces.

Nobody could challenge Ivan's wanton supremacy. On one occasion the head of the orthodox church pleaded for mercy to be shown towards some men accused of rebelliousness. Not only did his pleas fall on deaf ears, but he too was arrested, charged with sorcery, tortured and killed. Russia under Ivan was not a place to raise one's head above any parapet, however low that protective wall might be.

❧ V ❧
THE SACKING OF
NOVGOROD, AND OTHER
CAMPAIGNS

«To shave the beard is a sin that the blood of all the martyrs cannot cleanse. It is to deface the image of man created by God.»

Ivan the Terrible

It was not even necessary to offer any opposition, however minor, to attract the attention of the tyrannical Tsar. The news that the city of Novgorod was planning to rebel was never more than an unsubstantiated rumor. Ivan needed no more. He already had his vindictive and paranoid eyes on the unproblematic settlement. A year before his ransacking of the city he had evicted numerous residents from both Novgorod and the adjacent town of Pskov on the off chance that there could be sedition within their city walls.

A couple of years before he had lost, then regained, the town of Izborsk, and was terrified that this was a sign of growing and widespread treason. His fears were based on nothing but misplaced instinct and neurosis.

Then, in the months leading up to the sacking, he executed Prince Vladimir and many of his family, He drowned Vladimir's mother and wife. It is perhaps more than a passing coincidence that many of Vladimir's surviving associates lived in Novgorod. The execution of the Prince was typical of Ivan's behavior during the latter part of the 1560s. Recovering from illness, he approached the Prince – who happened to also be his cousin and gave him the honor of becoming his own son's regent in the event of his death.

But something changed his attitudes towards Vladimir, and in 1569 the executions took place. No further explanation was forthcoming. Except, perhaps, that Ivan was simply mad.

AN UNNECESSARY REVENGE - NOVGOROD

In 1570 he ordered his oprichnik to attack the city. The attack does not do justice to the ferocity of their campaign of terror. For five weeks, the secret police sacked the city, massacring, capturing, torturing, raping the inhabitants. Nobody was safe. From the youngest peasant baby to the matriarch of a local Boyar. All were subject to random, unjustifiable cruelty. The attack has entered, for all the wrong reasons, into the folklore of Russian culture. It was immortalized in Tchaikovsky's opera, '*The Oprichnik*,' and Vasnetsov's painting, '*The Street in the Town*.'

If there was to be a justification for his attack, and Ivan did like to be able to explain away the excesses of his behavior, it was that the city's Boyars were planning to hand it over to the expanding Polish and Lithuanian Commonwealth, itself a sworn enemy of Ivan. Their seditious act was to be aided by Bishop Pimen, the archbishop of the city.

However, it seems that there was little evidence to support this theory, although some historians believe that agents of the commonwealth may have planted papers to destabilize the tsar (a condition which, it is safe to say, was already well underway.)

On 6th January, Ivan arrived outside the city with fifteen-year-old Ivan and some 1500 troops. He ordered that senior clergy member and monks be rounded up, and these were executed on the following day, beaten to death before being returned to their monasteries for burial.

On the 8th, Ivan the Terrible advanced to the Volkhov river, where he was met by the Archbishop. This was a traditional courtesy extended to senior members of society and, still the following convention, an attempt was made by Pimen to bless his tsar. The gesture was rebuffed, and instead Ivan made his accusation of treachery against the churchman, and in turn, the city.

But we see the disturbed state of Ivan's mind through what happened next. He demanded to be taken to the cathedral so that he could take divine liturgy. Later, he insisted on being hosted by the Bishop. Each of the above took place within the chaos of a pillaging raid. Pimen was arrested as their meal began, his residency was plundered, and the Archbishop publicly humiliated.

For something he would try to justify as a religious and political cleansing, Ivan's actions seemed to be more tied to financial gain than might be expected. Churches, cathedrals and monasteries were stripped of their treasures.

Operating on the principle that great fortunes are built on pennies, he even ordered city clergy to be flogged until they handed over the sum of twenty rubles.

While the improvised court at the tsar's make do Gorodische camp was beginning to wind down – there are only so many officials to try and execute – the ransacking of wealth from the city continued unabated, with Ivan himself frequently overseeing the work of his oprichniki. What could not easily be stolen away was demolished; church bells were cast to the floor, cattle were slaughtered, church elders were punished just because they could be.

But as bad as the stripping of the city's assets might be, it was the treatment he conducted against the city's inhabitants that most horrifies, still so more than four centuries on. Some of this wickedness was directed against specific members of the Boyars and the middle classes. At other times, there took place simply a generic slaughter of the peasantry.

❦

False confessions were given under torture, implicating other innocent people in the treason Ivan claimed to suspect. Torture included being grilled over a giant frying pan type device; others were hung by their hands, and their eyebrows singed away.

❦

Young children were thrown into the freezing Volkhov river. There patrolling oprichniki waiting with spears and lances pushed any that managed to surface back under the cracked ice.

❦

When the trials had finished, propelling several hundred nobles, statesmen and clergymen to a painful and untimely death, the oprichniki opted for a quicker route to increasing the tsar's coffers while simultaneously crushing any lingering thought of rebellion.

❦

Houses were pillaged and destroyed, along with any inhabitant who might object. Often, when the mood took him, an oprichniki would simply kill a homeowner, or their children, for the simple pleasure of doing so. These decisions could be justified as pressing home the lesson of the futility of opposing the tsar (not that, in any case, these people were considering such an action). At other times, residents were randomly dragged before Ivan so that he could practice his sadistic forms of torture, with his son watching on the sidelines.

❧

In all, it is thought that 15000 people died as a direct result of the sacking of Novgorod. Countless more perished because their homes were destroyed, and they were forced out into the unforgiving Russian winter, with no shelter to protect them from the snow, ice and bitter winds. Figures for the total number of deaths which resulted from the attack range from 10000 to 60000 all told. The lower number is based on the fact that the city had recently suffered famine and outbreaks of disease, so the population was low anyway. The higher figure uses the typical number of the city's inhabitants.

❧

It is sad that, when each death represents the suffering of a person and the snuffing out of existence, records are so imprecise.

❧

As was his wont, Ivan lost interest a few days into the slaughter, taking an increasingly back seat, but the oprichniki continued their suppression until mid-February before moving on to similar invasions of other cities. The tsar's rule was perhaps the most sadistic in the known history of mankind, and the destruction of Novgorod its most excessive deed.

If the horror of Novgorod teaches us anything we did not already know about this barbarous tyrant, it is an insight into his need to justify his actions. There can surely be no doubt that, while the slaughter was happening, he was thrilled by the torture, pain, and suffering he inflicted on his frequently innocent victims. But it was equally important to Ivan that he could be justified in his cruel actions.

He needed confessions. He needed to know that his actions were a fitting punishment for one who strayed. And he would inflict whatever pain was necessary to draw those confessions. It is a bizarre scenario; a man causing the most unimaginable degrees of pain to a person to draw the words that vindicate the infliction of that suffering.

We see in Ivan the paranoia, the psychotic behavior of the sociopath. He enjoys inflicting suffering but must also rationalize his conduct in doing this. He must believe that his actions are right and proper in the eyes of God. It is delusional behavior, enacted by one who knows no boundaries, and on whom no boundaries can be imposed.

ON TO MOSCOW

❦

Novgorod was not alone in feeling the ire of a leader out of control. Moscow suffered too, as did the town of Pskov. Fearing opposition to his actions in Novgorod, he targeted the moderate noblemen of the city. A mass trial followed.

❦

Its outcome was never in doubt. Under his recently constructed cathedral in Red Square, eighteen scaffolds were erected. Near them, alarmingly, was situated a large cauldron. It was filled with water, and beneath it, a large fire was lit.

❦

Once more, Ivan needed his audience. Moscovites had fled at the site of the preparations, but now they were rounded up and dragged to the square to witness the bloodbath about to ensue. Hundreds were executed on the first day of the witch hunt alone. Members of the army, of the state, of the Boyars – all could be targets. Playing to his crowd, Ivan demonstrated he could be benevolent as well as fearsome. He approached the terrified captives and extended his benign forgiveness, pardoning around 180 of the terrified prisoners.

According to records, the first to die was a statesman called Viskoyati. Ivan struck him powerfully on the head as he read out each trumped-up charge. Viskoyati screamed his loyalty and innocence, but it was to no accord. He was strung upside down and his ear cut off. Then slowly, painfully his body was hacked to pieces, a limb at a time until he could scream no more. The second victim to be hauled forward was a friend of Viskoyati; the town treasurer, Funikov-Kartsev.

He was subjected to the same treatment as his now deceased pal. And so, it continued, the crowd baying its support, caught up in a mixture of blood lust combined with fear for doing anything but offer clear and vocal support for their Tsar.

When the pleasures of killing men began to wane, Ivan allegedly taunted the remaining terrified prisoners. Then he traveled to the families of his victims, to gloat some more. The story goes that when he arrived at the home of the wealthy former treasurer, Funikov-Kartsev, he tortured the dead man's wife, the better to ensure he could seize all her goods. He then turned his attention to her daughter, whom he handed over for the pleasure of his son. Both were just fifteen years of age.

Later, the giant cauldron was employed to boil his victims until the flesh fell from their bones and they screamed for the end of their suffering. No doubt, while this was happening, Ivan himself was in turmoil. His crazed mind would be switching between the ecstasy that watching such suffering brought, a sense of justification for the rightfulness of his actions, a pious joy for acting in the manner of his own interpretation of his God's wishes, and simple satisfaction that his power was being more and more embedded in the lifeblood of his petrified nation. Later would come the guilt, followed by the penance he enacted upon himself, beating his own body while prostrate before some religious icon or other.

Then the self-justification that he was acting out the will of his God would return. And with it, once more the need to torture and murder further innocent victims.

If the slaughters of Moscow lacked the scale of Novgorod, nevertheless they are still at the most end of man's inhumanity to man.

It is hard to imagine the reasons for such barbarity. But it seems as though, to Ivan, his punishments were justified by God – they reflected his interpretation of the bible. The problem for those he targeted was that this was the Bible interpreted by a madman. Added to this is the fact that Ivan simply enjoyed inflicting pain. He had done so as a child on the innocent animals he flung from the high windows of his palace and that thrill of causing pain had continued. But it had needed to become ever more severe for him to be satisfied by his fix.

The only break from the catalog of pain he caused fell during the short period of his marriage to Anastasia.

HEADING FOR DEFEAT – THE
LIVONIAN WAR

❧

I t is of no surprise that much of the tsar's time as leader
of Russia was spent at war with one opponent or other.
We have heard of his ongoing conflict with the Tartar
armies. The other great battle in which he engaged was the
Livonian war.

❧

Once the Volga had been secured, Ivan sought access to the
west. He believed that a safe route to the Baltic sea would
help him to secure stronger trading relations with the wealthy
markets of western Europe.

❧

Unfortunately, Livonia (which is located in what is today
Latvia and Estonia) stood in the way. Early in the campaign,
Russia made some successful incursions into a foreign land,

but the Livonian's allies Lithuania and Poland came to their aid. Then Sweden joined in on the opponent's side. Seeing their traditional enemy under pressure, the Tartars attacked from the Crimean, even reaching as far as Moscow. They set the city on fire, the Kremlin being one of the few buildings to remain undamaged.

The Livonian war lasted for an astonishing twenty-four years and only ended when Ivan began to realize that defeat faced him. He sought arbitration from Pope Gregory XIII. The head of the Catholic church agreed and sent his emissary, Antonio Possevino to arrange an armistice.

Ivan held on to power in his homeland, but at a price. He was forced to give up all his gains in Livonia, and hand over some towns in the Gulf of Finland. For a man with the pride of Ivan, this was humiliation in the extreme. And, of course, it was his people who paid the penalty.

THE FALL OF THE OPRICHNIKI

❦

No papers exist recording the exact details of the oprichniki. Most probably, they were created to aid Ivan as he fought against Boyars who resisted his reforms.

❦

Although they have an infamous role in Russian history of the era, the oprichiniki only lasted for seven years, from 1565 to 1572.

❦

Ivan blamed them for failing to prevent the attack of the Crimean Tartars on Moscow. Heads rolled, literally, and many of the houses, treasures and much of the land they had confiscated were returned to their original owners.

But despite the brevity of their reign, nothing can diminish the horror this secret army imparted on the Russian people. Their existence coincided with the most barbarous part of Ivan's time as tsar. The fury, anger, and madness that re-emerged following the death of Anastasia was to the fore, but he also possessed the wellness of body (mostly) and emotional energy to carry out the worst extremes of his brutal rule.

It is of no surprise that this period matched the time of the oprichiniki's predominance.

ꙮ VI ꙮ
DEATH

"I am a Christian and do not eat meat in Lent."

Ivan the Terrible

Eventually, inevitably, the tsar's vicious temper got the better of him. In 1581 an argument burst out between his son Ivan's wife and him, during which he abused her. To be blunt, he beat her up. Violently. So violently that she miscarried the child and heir, she was carrying. Ivan did the unthinkable and stood up against his father.

DEATH OF A FAVORITE SON

❧❧❧

E ven though he idolized his son more than anybody still living on earth, Ivan the Terrible struck out with his staff, causing a deep wound to his son's head. The younger man collapsed. He lingered on for several days before becoming yet another victim of his father's wickedness and uncontrollable temper. Albeit, this time an unintended one. It was an act from which Ivan would never recover.

❧❧❧

Feodor, the tsar's other son, became the heir. But he was weak, incompetent and childless. Ivan saw not only the death of his favorite son but also of his part of the Rurik dynasty. This would now, he feared, become no more than a short-lived deviation in his country's history and of the house of Rurik's lengthy reign.

He was wracked by guilt and consumed by grief. And that made, if possible, his paranoia worse. His already feeble grasp on reality seemingly collapsed altogether. He appealed to Queen Elizabeth the First of England for asylum. In a desperate attempt to both assuage his guilt and justify his excessive behavior, he drew up long lists of those he had executed. They would be very long lists indeed.

Having robbed the monasteries of their wealth just a few years before, now he paid them to say prayers on his behalf – anything to address his guilt. He even, as his death approached, ordered that he be rechristened. He chose to spend the last few months of his life reborn as a monk.

DEATH OF A DICTATOR

༶✿༶

Ivan was fifty-four years old when he died. He was playing chess when he collapsed. His opponent was one of the few men whom he trusted, his bodyguard Bogdan Belsky. It is believed that Russia's first tsar succumbed to a stroke. His orders were that he was to be buried wearing his monk's habit in a final desperate attempt to achieve God's forgiveness. He had no wish to spend his eternity in the hell to which he was surely destined.

A LEGACY LOST

❧

For the few short years of his marriage to Anastasia, Ivan had begun the process of bringing Russia together and making it a great nation. But he spent the final decades of his life tearing that legacy apart.

❧

The Moscow he left behind was destitute, broken and in chaos. A huge void filled the hole his despotic life had left. Russia was a much larger country than the one in which he had seized power as a boy all those years ago, but despite its geographical greatness, its resources were stretched, it was vulnerable to attack, and its people were downtrodden and afraid. Indeed, the entire future of Russia lay on a knife edge.

❧

Perhaps, though, one positive came from Ivan the Terrible's

reign. Such was his manic devotion to God that he ordered the building of a great colossus, which became the magnificent Moscow monolith that is St Basil's cathedral. It served as a shrine to his great achievements, notably the capture of Kazan.

Supposedly, so the story goes, Ivan was so moved by the magnificent building that he ordered its architect, Postnik Yakovlev, to be blinded so that no more beautiful building could ever be created by him.

Neat as that story might be, it is probably untrue. An exaggeration carried on the numerous myths surrounding the great tyrant. Yakovlev is credited with the design of numerous other religious and royal buildings in the years to come, which is a difficult achievement for a blind man to craft.

Despite the suggestion of religious worship in the name of this edifice, St Basil's was no more than a physical expression of Ivan's egocentricity. It became a temple to himself, living its life behind the mask of being a shrine to God.

❧ VII ❧
CONCLUSION

✦

Is there very much we can say in Ivan the Terrible's favor? It's pretty difficult to find many positives to take from this man and hold up as an example of how we might choose to live our lives.

✦

He was committed to his beliefs and faith in God. We might argue that such spiritual fortitude is a worthy attribute. Unfortunately, Ivan's faith was extreme and weighted with his own vastly unjustifiable interpretation of the wishes of his God. In light of this, we might conclude that his devotion was more of a selfish action than one seeking to lead him towards the attainment of higher levels of spirituality.

✦

His excessive prayers, his hours of sermonizing and the physical harm he caused himself and others in those endless mornings with his Oprichniki were a way of justifying his sadistic streak. They sought to excuse the guilt his excesses caused him. They were not the actions of a devoted monk, or indeed any man of God we might recognize as such.

❦

Ivan was an intelligent man. He was well read, a composer and a poet of considerable skill. Somewhat bizarrely a piece of music he wrote achieved its place in the music department of the Russian Hall of Fame. Stichiron No. 1 in Honor of St. Peter was an orthodox liturgical hymn. In 1988 a recording of it became the first CD released in his country.

❦

However, it is somewhat difficult to balance the recording of one obscure piece of religious music against the slaughter of tens, maybe hundreds, of thousands who died directly as a result of the first Tsar's actions.

❦

What we can learn from Ivan the Terrible's life is a lesson of what can happen when certain unpleasant characteristics and events combine. His existence was the result of a recipe which contained the most undesirable mixture of ingredients.

❦

He inherited the genes of a line of leaders who were, to a

greater or lesser extent, tyrannical themselves; he grew up as an orphan; he was exposed to almost no love or affection during his childhood years; he possessed a cruel streak which enjoyed causing pain to others – human or animal; he almost certainly suffered from paranoid psychoses; he suffered further tragedy when his wife, whom he loved so dearly, died in mysterious circumstances. Finally, he possessed the absolute power and wealth to do exactly as he wished, with no-one to provide any kind of check or balance to his actions.

❧

The result of these characteristics was the decimation of a nation. Today, it is easy to see Ivan becoming a person such as Ted Bundy, or Charles Manson, or Fred West. Andrei Chikatilo, the Butcher of Rostok, shared many of the childhood experiences Ivan endured – lack of food, care, exposure to scenes of frightening violence. But, unlike Ivan, he did not inherit control of his nation, and his murders were limited to between fifty and a hundred (he was convicted of fifty-two counts of murder, although was probably guilty of many more.)

❧

Hitler, Pol Pot, Ceausescu were modern dictators in his mold. Given the differences in technology available to these despots in the twentieth century compared to the sixteenth, even their atrocities do no match those of Ivan the Terrible.

❧

If we can learn anything from Ivan's life, it is a confirmation that bad childhoods can lead to bad adults; that unrestricted power corrupts; that man can hold the darkest of hearts. But they are not new lessons; nevertheless, they can never too often be restated.

❧ VIII ❧
FURTHER READING

❦

Those readers whose interest in this dictator has been sparked, the following three books offer further insights into his actions and character:

- Ivan the Terrible by Isabel D Madariaga
- Ivan the Terrible by Robert Payne and Nikita Romanov
- Fearful Majesty: The Life and Reign of Ivan the Terrible by Benson Bobrick

YOUR FREE EBOOK!

As a way of saying thank you for reading our book, we're offering you a free copy of the below eBook.

Happy Reading!